ANTHROVERATION

BY

LARRY A. YFF

CHAPTERS

1. Intro To Anthroveration

2. In The Beginning

3. A New Day

4. Study The Process

5. Understand Your Purpose

6. Write The Vision

7. Live The Dream

ACKNOWLEDGEMENTS

I have to thank God in the Bible for giving me this opportunity.

I want to thank my parents, Bob and Annette Yff, for listening to God's call and adopting me.

I want to thank the television pastors and teachers of the Bible that made the Word available to me in the privacy of my home when my faith was not strong in myself or in the church. Their messages allowed me to build my faith at my own pace.

Those of you who are reading this and know your role in our modern day gentrification of inner cities and want to gain new perspective or if you want to see if your perspective is justified...I thank and applaud you for taking a step. A step towards proper perspective is a step towards gaining proper perspective.

Those of you who are reading this and are seeking clarity to all the rumors and rumblings about gentrification...I thank and applaud you as well for taking a step. A step towards clarity is a step towards gaining clarity.

To those of you who have are feeling the weight and frustration of gentrification, you will find relief soon because when you read all the way through this book and get to the last page...that will be the first page in your new story that you are writing and in control of.

We are all humans and we all have value. To us!!

CHAPTER ONE

Intro to Anthroveration

Our communities have buildings and structures that have fallen into disrepair but are being renovated and given facelifts at a remarkable pace considering. I say "considering" because if these communities had access to the flow of millions of dollars that now infiltrate every block, those areas would never have seen the levels of deterioration at the rate that they have.

The cultural group that characterizes me the most is African American. When I use the words "our" and "we" in the context of this manuscript I am referring to any and all human beings. Looking at this situation from any other perspective is not proper and would critically limit our capacities as players in the solution, rendering us as mere side-liners in the spectator's seats.

Anyone who understands "white flight" and the "great black migration" that both took place in the twentieth century knows that our cities have been thrown into disarray because we allowed our morality to be divided and decided along cultural lines; and we have erroneously chosen to either use or withhold financial investment resources based along these same lines into our cities and the results are unacceptable and intolerable.

Even if neither of those terms is familiar to you, the dynamics of those events are shaping and have shaped every area of your life as you know it today without you even knowing it. To continue in that fashion would continue to give our country the intentionally disastrous and morally corrupt conditions we are seeing today.

Gentrification came along like a wolf in sheep's clothing and disguised itself as "the urban answer" only to have its true nature revealed which is "the corruptor of the classes" with those directly involved proudly wearing that title on their sleeves. However, within every labeled section of society there are those who have unwittingly become a part of a class without understanding why they are often being vilified for simply enjoying their lives as is their natural right. If this is you, you will find both the answer and the solution in this book.

As a human being, I cannot sit by and watch while investment profits, often controlled within cultural lines, continue to be the deciding factor of gentrification as to who deserves to have a decent quality of life in our cities and who gets kicked out of the nest.

I would like to offer you a very real solution to this very real and disturbing situation that gentrification has created. A solution that distributes wealth with blind and equal efficiency and profitability to those deserving and in the know how. A solution that has no concerns over the cultural make up or financial class of any given community...in fact, this solution thrives on verifying, validating and incorporating the various aspects of different cultures into its revitalization efforts. A solution that any of us who want to participate in can do so right now. There is a solution that requires no degree or investment capital to be effective. A solution that at its most fundamental core was designed "by we the people for the benefit of we the people to pursue love, life and happiness here on Earth."

<u>Anthroveration</u> is that solution.

Anthroveration (an-throw-ver-ration): noun; the faith-based process of structuring and prioritizing any given community accompanied with the application of anthropology.

- Literal meaning: human, verify, action.
- In a sentence: *Christian* anthroveration *has significantly curbed the number of involuntarily displaced residents in our city.*
- Anthrovert: noun; one who practices or fundamentally agrees with anthroveration.
- Anthroverate: -ed; action verb; *we need to* anthroverate *City X; City X was partially* anthroverated *in 2017 and the city's economic base has seen massive growth.*

Understanding what anthroveration is and how it works will change every area of your life; changing your view on your role, accountability and purpose on this planet. No longer will you want to be a part of a system that offers you any type of "privilege" without inquiring who was footing the bill. Ask for a receipt. Pay your fare. THAT is true, human privilege in this life: having the freedom and the ability to enjoy life without interfering with someone else's pursuit of happiness while protecting the rights and privileges of others to do the same in their own way.

    We all get there at different times in our lives. That calm place. That place where our inner self has a confidence that can only be explained by the supernatural. Some credit meditation while others call it being one with the Universe. As a Christian, I call it being filled with the Holy Spirit and He has begun to mold me into an unstoppable force for justice; pulling wealth, creativity and truth into my orbit as I continue to learn how to harness Its power.

    The more I "got there", the more my views and perspectives changed. As I reached towards spiritual and mental clarity I now had a moral obligation to take action. What will you do when you "get there?" What will your story be? This is the story of how I got there:

CHAPTER TWO

In The Beginning

As a part of a group mailing, I began to get daily email alerts from my big sister in Texas. They were emails that had a Bible verse and a word of encouragement in it. At first I would just pass over them until one of them caught my eye. Which one it was I am not sure.

At the same time that I was getting these emails, I had decided I needed to start going to church. My daughter in Texas told me that I had to go. So I put on some clean jeans and a button up shirt and was at the early morning service fairly bright-eyed and bushy-tailed.

Something about the combination of regularly attending church while I was regularly reading those emails energized me. It was a good feeling knowing that I was making a conscious effort to do something that was good for me and I was kind of doing it on my own.

By "on my own" I mean that I was fairly irresponsible and my success in life up to that point was following behind my big brother in Detroit or my big sister in Texas. I didn't have confidence in my own ability to run a business even though I would get the itch to do that.

There were times where I wanted to tell my brother that we should try doing business a different way, but his way was working for us for now and we were both content. We had visions of how to take it to the next level, but life had a way of keeping us on a certain path.

I had a chance to get into a rather large business deal in Texas after meeting a lady and I decided it would be best if I just introduced her to my sister because my sister was good at business and she thrived on starting new companies and new ventures. In fact, I came across a couple of other business ventures that I absolutely believed in but I decided to introduce them to my sister. There was one that my sister had me involved in and I loved and had some great ideas to expand, but one of her managers abruptly decided to cut me out of all decision-making and fired me from the project.

My big brother and sister did the best they could with me. They both knew I was dealing with addiction to cocaine but didn't know on what level. I was still reliable enough to get a job done, but not reliable enough to manage any type of project over a long period of time. They had both given me multiple chances to step my game up, but I allowed my addiction and wild ass attitude to get in the way with the end of my Teas rope being when I caught a small case for threatening somebody, I had spent most of my money in strip clubs getting high and I got mixed up with some boys that were into home invasions. I had to do better.

They also knew I had stretched myself thin family-wise with kids in different cities and they would verbally express, or imply, that I should work on being a good dad and maybe that would settle me down. Both of them were all about taking care of family and their responsibilities and if I wasn't family, they probably would have kicked me off their teams years ago.

My newly gained confidence in myself began to kick in a little bit at a time now and I wanted to step out on my own more and more. Just how and when and where I didn't know, but I knew I had to step out sooner than later. The disappointments in myself and the fact that I wanted to do my own thing was eating at me on a daily basis now.

I would eventually leave Texas and my big sister to head back to Detroit with my big brother. I told myself that I would not get involved with my sister in business anymore until I was able to do it responsibly and productively and on a consistent basis. That conscious decision and sticking with it gave me another little boost and a sense that I was heading in the direction of being "on my own" and I kind of liked it.

Upon arriving back in Detroit, my big brother and I got back into the same working groove that we were accustomed to. As usual, he had to get the jobs and negotiate the pay for us and he had to have the transportation and he had to have the house for us to live in and take care of most of the bills...I had none of those things nor the notion to rush and get myself into a better position at that time.

I was just enjoying myself and Detroit. As was my cycle in life, I had a couple of cases for stolen cars there over the last several years there and I was still getting high on cocaine and was a bodyguard of sorts for a close friend of mine. I knew I had to make a change, but the "how" was the part I wasn't grasping. I did know that it somehow had to do with me returning to church and getting some kind of Bible in me during the week and not just for an hour on Sunday.

Leaving Detroit, I moved to Muskegon Heights and lived with my son and his mother for a while. For a minute I got back into my old groove of doing a job and blowing the money or not being able to keep a steady paying job.

I seemed more and more aware that I had to use this new concept of making conscious choices to make a change in my life and I decided to make another one. I decided that I would not work with my big brother anymore either until I was able to operate as equals and be responsible. Standing by that choice gave me another small boost that I was able to make decisions and keep them. I hadn't seen much financial gain or a change in my lifestyle, but the seed had been planted and now enough drops of water had been dropped around it making the ground fertile for more growth.

It was here that I met an older lady who would become my grandmother figure and also a mentor when it came to doing business. Ciggzree Morris is her name and when I met her, she was around 70 years old, out and about every day taking care of business and making plans to revitalize entire cities like she was 30-something years old. She never stopped. I admired that in her and also her regular attendance of church to the point where I became a member there.

She had made several milestones in her lifetime in the area of business and real estate. Being able to call her my close friend and family member gave me yet another boost. I had now made the decision to be a member at a church I liked, began to pay my tithes fairly consistently and had a friend in Ciggzree that was a good influence in every way. I hadn't had a friend/mentor like her before and it felt good and motivated me.

The opportunity came for me to operate as equals with my big brother. A big electrical and plumbing job came up and I knew he could get it done. I reached out to him and he agreed. I was in Detroit with him for a weekend visiting my daughters and I drove back with him to Muskegon Heights to start the job. On the highway heading there this young lady swerved into me as we were going along a curve and I tried to steady the truck but couldn't. We slid across the other lane onto the grassy median and then slammed into the guardrail tearing up at least twenty feet of it before spinning around out of control before sliding to an abrupt stop.

When the police came on the scene, they asked me for my information since I was the driver. I had a suspended license so they took me from the scene of the crash straight to jail. After spending a couple of days there I was transferred to Kent County Jail[1] to do time for not keeping up with my child support payments. It was there that God had me get ready to kick it up a notch.

Before I go further I have to add something. This accident put my life on a totally different path. If it were not for that accident, I would not have come across the people that I needed to come across that were monumental to my change when I did. You may not believe this, but something in my soul told me an angel had a hand in the accident. I was listening to the young lady

---

[1] To be as accurate as possible, the actual times that I was in jail all blurred together; regardless, my enlightenment occurred during one of those times.

talk that had crashed into me and I heard her say "I don't know what happened. It felt like somebody had grabbed my steering wheel and the next thing you know I crashed into that guy's truck…" I didn't know it then, but that accident would prove to definitely be one of thee most pivotal points in my transformation process.

So now, post-accident, I am in the county jail. The first thing I requested was a Bible. I am in solitary confinement and had no one to talk to so I decided that I would use the next couple of months wisely and make a conscious decision to keep the faith and do my daily reading like I had gotten accustomed to. This time would prove to put my mind on a whole new level.

CHAPTER THREE

A New Day

I began my Bible reading a little bit every day. The Holy Spirit had led me to the Joseph story first. This story completely turned my business brain on because of his rise in the political and business world. Joseph had a vision that he would somehow be a great ruler, but it took years and years to come true and during this time he had many ups and downs including being in slavery and locked up in prison. I had the same feeling that I would be extremely great and productive on a level that had not been seen before, but I wasn't sure in what areas it would be.

I remember that while I was reading his story, as something would stand out to me, I would stop reading and actually go through what I would say if I was going to preach on that point that I came across. That one story of Joseph led me to speak about six different sermons that were each about thirty minutes long. I had never done anything like that before in my life. The excitement while I was "preaching" gave me a new kind of high. I was laughing at the humor I placed in the sermons and it felt like I was taking in every drop of information I was preaching about and it was feeding my soul somehow.

This continued off and on throughout the next several days. I began to recite sermons off the top of my head from reading about all the different stories. Each story resulted in another sermon.

These moments were mixed in with thoughts of my children. I had thoughts of the reality of how bad of a father I was to them all. It was during these days that I would begin to cry and shake uncontrollably as I thought of the pain they must have had as they watched me abandon them time and time again, or the disappointment they must have felt when I didn't show up for important things like their first tooth coming in or falling out. I just sat and admitted what I had done and then the tears would flow uncontrollably.

Those were very long days...very long, heavy and emotionally draining days. I would try and control my emotions but I would vacillate from anger to sadness to depression and then return full circle to rage at being in jail again. Those days acted as an introduction into a soul searching process that would shatter my self-image and force me to change my view of myself and my purpose.

Somehow though, I felt God telling me it was okay to let my emotions go. It was okay to admit how I was an awful daddy. It was okay because in order to get to the next level, I had to take a look at myself and deal with myself. In the past I would just live carefree and not deal with emotions or if I got emotional I would get high or somebody would get hurt. I usually leaned towards getting high because to me there was less damage done considering I could get locked up for life for resorting to violence.

So now my days alternate with the sermon days and the emotional days. The Bible says God always has plans for your good and as I began to cry my pains and shame away in the physical, my mental began to get stronger. I was now making conscious decisions to picture my one of my kids crying because I wasn't around, and as I imagined it, I faced the fact that I wasn't there and eventually I learned to say "I can't go back in the past but I have to make better choices for my future so I don't put my children through this anymore" and I was content with that. I was actually being able to see how I could be a part of God's plan.

In fact, my "sermons" began to get more personal. I found myself incorporating situations I had gone through that were similar to some of the guys in the Bible. Something about being able to openly talk about it and picture doing that in front of people gave me a sense of power. Not "pulpit power", but a power that I am not bound by certain shackles of shame and guilt and that I was somehow helping others get un-bound with my testimonies and sermons.

Around this same time I began to hear the Holy Spirit give me different ideas about business. I am not sure which idea came first, but I remember in one week's time I had around seven business ideas and concepts that to this day I have pretty much memorized. I do know one of the first ones dealt with real estate. The real estate development of an entire city, Muskegon Heights, was one of the first ones, to be exact.

It began with me imagining I could buy a couple of houses from the city's auction or tax foreclosure list and begin to flip them for a nice profit. From there, the real estate development thing took on a life all its own.

I had begun to imagine buying all the houses on the auction list. I even had written the letter detailing out how I could go about doing it and the benefit it would have to the city. When

I told God that that would be a lot of money, He said "All the money on this planet is under my control. I give it to who I want and take it from who I want. So if your plan is to use it for My glory, I will make sure you have more than you need to do so." That answer was good enough for me.

Now I had plans enter my head not only about the exact way each house would get renovated to maximize the community's assets, I began to have plans for the abandoned lots. Then I had plans for certain businesses I had seen around town. Each building and set of empty lots began to take on a purposeful form, not only in the process of buying them but also in the process of developing them.

Then the thought of buying a certain hotel there came to mind. I wrote the plans for how it would look on the inside and out and how I would market it. That's when I got very excited and said to God, "I really feel these plans in my heart and I'm excited, but now these plans are costing into the millions for real...and not just a couple of million." God replied to me, not in an irritated voice because I had already expressed concern about how I would get that kind of money, but with a tone so sure that it gave me 100% confidence that I would somehow have all the financial resources I would need for every single project I envisioned.

He said, "You have the heart for people and your interest is not in just making money. Your excitement from these projects will all be extremely profitable and you can see it, but that is not what is exciting you. What is exciting you is that you now can see why you have gone through a lot of the things you have in life and now you feel like you will be able to do business from your heart and because of that, you do not have to worry about a thing. You are looking for all the right answers and I am giving them to you. Continue to write down any plan that comes to mind and do not even think about the cost at all."

I remembered feeling a weird and complete calm. I used the term "weird" because at that point remember, I had no money to my name. I had a suspended driver's license and no real job. When I would work, I would spend a good portion of it on drugs and entertainment. But all that didn't matter. When God told me I would have everything I needed, I felt it in my core. I felt it in every single molecule in my body. I had an absolute confidence and I knew it would happen. I actually remember laughing in excitement like "This is for real!!"

So we have real estate development, and from that came different concepts for a development process that was centered on people...not profit. I began to see how to incorporate the local schools, non-profits, local businesses, churches and residents of all ages and education levels to accomplish the dream.

It was as if I was able to take a city and put all the pieces together based on Bible principles that were common sense. I could see the massive amount of money to be made, yes, BUT I saw how simple it was to achieve that without being greedy and by helping everyone else get what they want!

Every single stage of development that I wrote down gave me peace and excited me as I pictured the lives that would be changed forever.

While I was writing down real estate development plans, it was like I saw another whole "sub-economy" that would need to be developed and controlled. The goal wasn't to corner the market on the cash flow. The goal was to make help a community structure their economy how they wanted to, but if I was to be involved, there were certain principles that had to be plugged into every minute detail of every operation to maximize the community's assets and give God glory. I began to see that this could be done in any situation regardless of the economic or racial climate because God said He would give me any and everything I need.

Now I began to write down plans on controlling the entire investment process for the development plans. I envisioned what companies I would need and which ones in the community I would utilize. As I saw all of this unfold in front of my eyes, I would stop and just walk around my cell in amazement.

I had spent many years in Detroit and Houston. My inner "eyes" now began to shift towards both of those cities. I began to recall certain areas I lived in or was familiar with and imagined my total real estate development plan in action in both of those cities.

Reading books helped me break up some of my time. I enjoyed writing all of these plans out and it didn't even seem like work; but I had to try and take my mind off it and do my Bible studying and just daydreaming.

Sometimes I would begin to think about my personal situation with my kids and child support. Those thoughts lead me to think about the political/social justice scene. I began to understand how the system works and where the government needs to be held accountable and where the individuals need to be held accountable as well.

   Now I began to write plans about changing the welfare/State aid system in America on the individual's side and the government's side. The finer points of these topics wouldn't come into play until I got out and began to have these "think tank" sessions in the world.

   Even the books I would read to relax my brain inspired me to write about my involvement in different areas. Getting involved in the judicial system correcting wrongs was next on my list. There were concepts and ideas I now wanted to work on dealing with constitutional law that really got me excited. Like I said though, some of these terms like "constitutional law" and "legal standing" didn't come to me in jail. The plans I would write regarding these ideas were skeleton outlines that got developed and technical once I got out and began to research each topic in depth.

   I would look at magazines and thoughts of entering the world of fashion began to come to me. Visions of having a fashion house that would be profitable, purposeful and known worldwide began to enter my brain. As usual, there was the main concept and then there was the whole sub-economy that I had plans to be involved in on multiple levels.

   Thoughts of all sorts of farming came to mind. Fish and shrimp, solar and agriculture farms all began to develop in my mind. When I got out of jail was where I would again begin to do more research and develop my skeleton outline in a way that would prove to be profitable and purposeful. The thing was that every single concept was somehow related to every other concept somehow. It was as though I had become an idea archaeologist discovering family ties and connections between multiple and seemingly unrelated business ideas that no one knew existed or had thought could all be so intricately related.

CHAPTER FOUR

Study The Process

The process is the proof. Studying the process helps you discover all the different aspects of the thing you want to be involved in. This concept is universal and applicable to sports, relationships, business dealings and any "thing" that you have decided to invest in.

With the calling on my life becoming clearer I had to really study the process for myself. My "thing" was my life. I had decided that I would live my life according to the Bible to the best of my ability. There were guidelines and rules for living that are just as relevant today as they were thousands of years ago when It was written. I knew the author of the Bible was God and that I wanted Him leading me and I needed to know how He operated.

Sharing the dream. I wanted to rise to power like Joseph. In studying his story I noticed that when he first had his vision, he shared it with his brothers and they all began to resent him. King David had a similar experience when a prophet of God, in front of all his brothers, anointed him to be the future king. The brothers were resentful and became his worst nightmare by beating him up and selling him into slavery. **I have a dream of greatness and I believe I have been anointed by God to accomplish it and I need 1) to be careful who I share it with because everyone won't see what you see and 2) some people who watch you rise may resent you for their own personal reasons.**

Networking for success. People today believe that the only way to be successful is to network. That has been the big thing: networking for success. Who you network with is more important than the number of networks you and are affiliated with.

While Joseph was in prison he told two royal officials what their dreams meant. He then told them to remember him when they got out and were working again for the king. As far as we know, that was the extent of his networking.

The Bible tells us that after the two officials got out, their dreams came true just like Joseph had said and the one who was still living had forgotten to tell the king about Joseph for several years, until the opportunity arose. The way that God worked in that scenario became my model for networking success: I don't have to base my success on who can connect me to the most money or people that are successful in their careers...I simply have to be able to see the vision God gave me and trust that when the time is right it will happen. What that does it alleviate a lot of stress and time wasted trying to convince people to believe in you and it also doesn't give you a warped sense of success.

People today are so busy rushing to convince people of their worth by trying to rub elbows with people who are rich or hold high business positions and finding mentors that can "lead them to success" that they have not tried to network with the one being that made this entire universe: God.

Joseph, David and other powerful leaders in the Bible had one person in their "connections file" and that's what took them to the top. They didn't waste their time looking for people to believe them or believe in them. **They understood the process and that is to keep focused on God and God will put the people you need in your life when the time is right for you to achieve whatever dream He has put on your heart.**

<u>**The process is a testing period for you.**</u> In every story of success that I read about in the Bible I saw that the process was insane! Some of the people had to go through prison first, some had to deal with rejection and isolation from their families and some had gone through some very hard times and made it through…only to be thrown back into more chaos! The story of Job is a classic example. Job was very wealthy and God allowed him to go through a process that you would have to read to believe. It involved his family dying and him enduring sickness on a level most of us cannot imagine.

In *every* story where the person went through a difficult process, their rewards were impressive! That's what I wanted and if that's what I wanted than I had to wrap my head around the fact that God is going to have to test me to see if I will crumble under pressure or if I will stand loyal to Him and keep my head up with the understanding that when the trial is over the testimony can begin.

I also saw that just because I endured one hard season doesn't mean they are all over. **Each season has its own lessons and if I want my road to success to be like the Men of God in the Bible, then I had to be ready to be tested by God and understand his testing process.**

<u>**Financing your dream.**</u> In this life we have a system of providing goods and services that is carried out through different

forms of money. You can borrow your way to a dream or be born into a family with wealth or you can create your own "life financing" by working a job or owning your own business...any way you slice it you will need to have some type of financing involved to make it happen.

Once again, in **every** Bible story where a Man of God rose to the power and positions that are also on my heart, I saw that **they never had to borrow a dime to get there**! They didn't have to try and work 90 hours a week at a job and deal with the frustration of not having enough time to enjoy life or having to get mad that they weren't making enough. **They understood that whatever job, position or predicament they were in was some sort of learning process and they threw themselves into with excitement and loyalty to God knowing that there was a plan to it by God somehow.**

By me understanding that key point in the process, I began to enjoy every job I had. During this time I had a couple of minimum wage jobs that I loved to go to because I was able to get money and show God how I could handle and budget a little bit and by doing that I knew He would get me into position to handle a lot...and I needed a lot to finance my dreams.

I didn't get caught up in complaining with some of my co-workers about not getting paid enough because I understood that if you are not in the mind frame to make wise choices with your money, it didn't matter if you made $7 an hour of $70 an hour. The results would be the same. I could have gotten frustrated, especially since child support payments were half of my paycheck but I didn't.

I had begun to understand the process of God's financing, the purpose and lessons learned from work and I focused on regularly tithing and using my "two's and few's" as wisely as possible…knowing this job wasn't the endgame to the financing of my calling.

CHAPTER FIVE

Understand Your Purpose

Every person's purpose is different. You have to find and feel in your heart what it is you like to do and find the best route to get there. If you never get the chance to follow your dream it gets frustrating and it shows in all areas of your life. The frustration comes out in how you deal with your kids or the jealousy of watching someone else achieve their goals can leave some of us bitter and resentful.

<u>Understanding your purpose.</u> After going through my incarcerated enlightenment period, I saw my purpose, I felt my purpose and I wanted to achieve my purpose…**not by any means necessary**…but to achieve it God's way.

I knew that my purpose was to change the business world, the political scene, the non-profit scene, the educational scene and every scene I came across. There is a difference though, in knowing one's purpose and understanding one's purpose. I knew my purpose, but as I looked around and talked with people, I couldn't understand it at first.

There were some things going on that I detested while most people were praising it. I saw lawyers who would knowingly represent a guilty person and instead of making sure the person got treated equally under the law as is their job, they were more interested in making a name for him or herself by twisting the law for a favorable outcome for their client! Even if it meant an admittedly guilty person would go free. But we are so conditioned to it that we consider it the norm. I even used to admire those lawyers because they were wealthy and considered respectable members in society. I wanted to be a lawyer at one time in my life.

We consider it normal for a person who sexually molests a child to have his lawyer fight to get his client's case dropped on a technicality; leaving the child's parents to take justice into their own hands...and then the parents end up serving 20 years in prison.

We see our politicians declare war with the clear understanding that their children, by laws that they made and approved, aren't going to be risking their lives on the front lines: it will be other parent's children getting killed or surviving only to not receive the proper medical care they need as is their right when they risked their lives to protect the rights of fellow countrymen they have never met.

We have all sat by and witnessed major corporations doing multi-billion dollar acquisitions while public schools around the world are getting closed because there is no available funding.

As a Christian, it has become the norm for me to see 30 churches in a city under the same umbrella of Christianity, yet not being able to or willing to get along because of difference of the interpretation of a line or two in the Bible.

I knew my purpose had to do with change but I was feeling as though I was becoming the guy that nobody wanted to talk about the latest news with because of my changing views on life. People would be all emotional about different reality show happenings as though it was all real life and I wasn't feeling that emotional rollercoaster ride that comes with watching those shows. I was the one who would say "Don't you see how fake and ignorant and staged those shows are?!? Don't you see how emotional you get after watching them??? Those shows are a complete waste of time and are for those who absolutely have not a thing better to do with their time" and that made me judgmental somehow and not a good Christian.

Or I would be the guy who, when a "major" issue about a white cop killing a black man was all over the news, didn't get emotional and mad at every white person on the planet. I began to take the view of "what is the root cause of people getting targeted and killed by police in certain areas?"...but that was considered wrong because I was black and I should get involved and stop acting like now that I publicly proclaimed my Christianity, I should be getting more involved in these issues "like a good Christian should instead of acting all holier than thou and not wanting to get involved."

As I watched people making decisions based on emotion, I began to understand how my purpose would need to unfold: it cannot be based on emotion. It was as though I could see that the devil's plan is to constantly keep people in a state of emotional instability with different events so that we are emotional and when you are emotional, decisions are not as decisive as they should be.

Have you ever noticed that there is a "hot topic of injustice" that is on every news channel and online venue for a couple of months...and then as the tempers cool down, another "major hot topic of injustice" always seems to pop up in some other part of the country and it starts all over again. Then there are the "all-important, hot-topic sex scandals" that get people all charged up and angry about. The timing of these un-newsworthy events seemed impeccable; as though they were achieving what I thought their goal was with pinpoint precision.

I began to feel more like an outsider the more I began to see what the real inside scoop was. It was as though God was pulling back the curtain and letting me see that the "great wizard of Oz, aka satan, is trying to use emotion instability to keep people unfocused on the real matters at hand, but as I would tell people this, they started acting like I was becoming too self-righteous when I was simply becoming more self-aware.

Now I was beginning to not only see what my purpose was and how I would go about doing it, I began to understand what my purpose was and how I would go about doing it.

As I felt mixed emotions and frustration, an anger rise inside of me, and I began to have absolute clarity as to what my purpose was on this planet: **My purpose was to apply lessons learned in the Bible with lessons learned from the studies of human nature, specifically the sub-categories of anthropology, to restructure and redefine cultures values and norms in a way that reflected and defined our human side without the prejudice of improper emotions in a more dignified manner...and thus the birth of "anthroveration".**

CHAPTER SIX

Write The Vision

Writing the vision. When you put the vision on paper, it serves as a daily reminder the game plan for bringing our vision to life. In the Bible it says that we should write down the plan as a means of providing clarity to a vision.

I had begun to get thoughts of many different business ideas in many different fields. Some of the ideas had 4 or 5 "sub-concepts" with them. Writing them all down in one book was essential for clarity for me as much as it was to have a written plan that I could share when the time came.

An example would be real estate. I had thoughts of dealing with hotels somehow, so the hotel concept was the main concept. From there, I had concepts for either starting a new boutique hotel chain or partnering with an existing chain. As I would ride to different cities I would see different aspects of different hotels that interested me.

The concept of adding a type of "family reunion park" to the hotel came next. The concept of having a skywalk with a mid-size arena followed and I began to draw basic floor plans for the hotel. That led to the concept of "time-sharing" hotel rooms and that led to a concept about what types of events I would have there and why. Then the concept for adding a "daycare/young people's level" came next.

This concept then expanded into an entire village complete with an educational building, movie theatre, boot-camp, gymnasium with dorms and athletic fields, apartment complexes for the workers and the athletic program participants, a joint-unit security office, a farm and a strip mall were also included.

For each of those hotel concepts came the "sub-concepts" which detailed how the individual programs would be structured and how I would market the program events.

As you can see, once God gives you a vision He also provides intel on every aspect of it that you need. It may be different for each person though. For some it may be very detailed and for others it may be a general idea.

For the two Bible people I mentioned earlier (King David and Joseph) they were given different styles for their life plans. For David it was simply that he would be King with no mention of how he would or should rule. For Joseph, he had a vision early on in life and then his opportunity came by giving instructions to the Egyptian king as to how the king should establish certain programs. The amazing thing is that **both of them became great rulers without formal education!** Understanding that is what gave me a greater understanding that God can work with me even though I may not have a college degree because I read about a style of His in the Bible where no formal education was needed.

That brings up a couple of important notes. In most all of the cases from the Bible God *never* told the person with the dream when it would happen and how long it would take. That is part of the excitement as a Christian because I know it will happen because God always keeps His word, but I don't know exactly what day things will begin to happen. It makes you face each new day, meeting or opportunity as though that may be the one to start the dream. I began to love Mondays!

Another important note is that it is an excellent idea to pursue more and more degrees...just don't make that your endgame. If you are basing the success of a plan that God gives you in wordly terms, you are subject to stress. Now you are focusing strictly on how everyone else said they got there and that is fine if you don't understand how God works or if you don't want Him to be the source of your success. But that is an unacceptable view if you want the advantage of the Holy Spirit guiding you to success. When you don't allow the supernatural force of faith in God guide you, here's what you are opening yourself up to: If you can't get the proper amount of financial aid: stress, depression, anxiety. If you can't find a baby-sitter so you can work more jobs or take more classes: stress, depression, anxiety. If you can't find two more jobs to help pay for the education and the training: stress, depression, anxiety. If you don't have the proper business networks that you think you have to have in order to accomplish your dreams: stress, depression, anxiety.

Understanding the process that you want to use to get you the success in life you desire will be one of the top three of the decisions you will make to ensure your success and significantly, if not eliminate, unnecessary stress, depression and anxiety. Writing the vision helps you get that clarity you need to see the direction your process will need to go.

CHAPTER SEVEN

Live The Dream

As of this writing, I have only just begun to live the dream on a level where I can show you proof of the process. I am sharing with you what a modern day, faith-based process looks like from the beginning. My dream involves the complete and total revitalization and restoration of any given community with the core of the process being faith-based and anthropology based. Its literal meaning is: a process of verifying humans based on faith-based principles and the study of anthropology.

This process is called anthroveration. In a way you can say it is designed to be an anti-gentrification system; but that would be giving gentrification too much credit. This process has enough dignity and humanity to stand on its own merit.

Anthroveration came about as a result of the inhumanity I had seen in gentrification. Gentrification places value in communities and on people based on economic and cultural factors, reducing people to numbers; while anthroveration believes that no community will exist without people and therefore, any and all efforts to prioritize the restoration and revitalization of the people in any given community is a must.

I look forward to implementing this process and sharing it with anyone who is interested. Whenever situations and events go against the grain of basic human rights and dignity...humans naturally make adjustments to correct it. Anthroveration is that natural adjustment!

Made in the USA
Lexington, KY
04 January 2018